CLIMATE CRISIS

CLIMATE CRISIS

Do Not Run Away

ARATI BORA BARUAH

Chandra Prakason

First Printing, September 4, 2023, USA
Climate Crisis, Do Not Run Away
Chandra Prakason
©2023 Arati Bora Baruah
Original edition, March 12th, 2023
Publisher - Chandra Kalita Prakason,
Zoo Road, Guwahati, India

General Reviewers:
Lenore Bailey
Dr. Avanti Bergquist
Carrie Cartwright Bergquist
Editing: Wandering Words Media
ISBN Hardbound 979-8-9881308-0-2
ISBN Paperback 979-8-9881308-1-9
ISBN E-book   979-8-9881308-2-6

First Printing, 2023

Dedication

To: Anjali, Anton, Zachary, Wes J, Charlotte, Evelyn, and the juveniles worldwide.

I have titled the book *Climate Crisis*, hoping that nature will regain balance for generations. Let us save tomorrow.

If you believe in Nature's Rebound, add your name here —

Contents

Climate Change: Author's Dilemma
Please read this first.

When I started working on a climate change book, I encountered quite a few practical issues. One is how much must I supply as reference papers or books? The most helpful information is available to the general public by internet search engines. Then we have ChatGPT4 not only to ask for facts but also some explanations. I think using ChatGPT this way is a good use of ChatGPT. I decided to do referencing a little differently. I realized I do not want to give references to the stuff that one can quickly obtain from reliable sources by searching the internet. For example, if you ask, "What are the Greenhouse Gases?" I do not think you can get a wrong answer from the internet.

Which gases are greenhouse gases? – Answer: Greenhouse gases comprise carbon dioxide, methane, ozone, nitrous oxide, chlorofluorocarbons, and water vapor.

However, if you want to know the connection between greenhouse gases, the Greenhouse Effect, and the warming of the climate, you may or may not get a proper

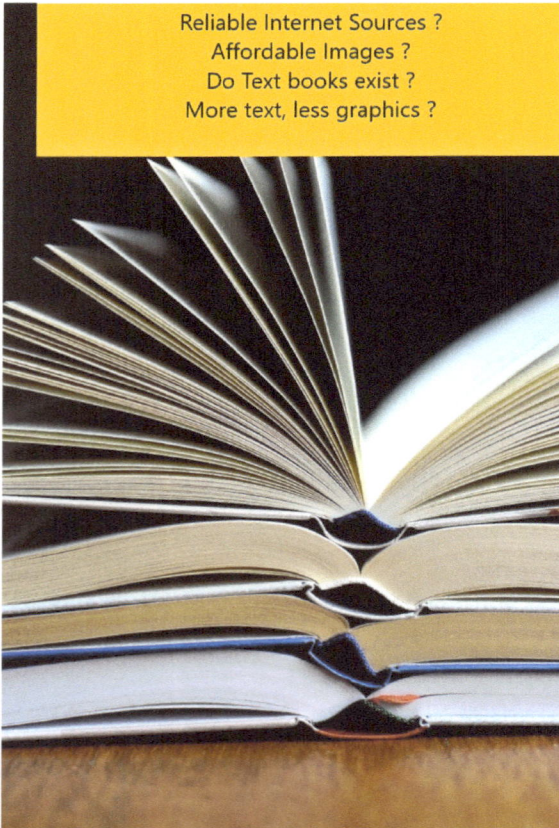

Reliable Internet Sources ?
Affordable Images ?
Do Text books exist ?
More text, less graphics ?

answer. I am explaining this to help the reader and students feel free to search for simple stuff if needed. I will explain my point with actual context precisely as I stumbled on it.

Human activities, i.e., the idea of human-caused climate change, emerged in the mid-1950s. Systematic measurement of the concentration of carbon dioxide in Earth's atmosphere led to the famous "Keeling Curve." It depicts a graph showing the ongoing change in the concentration of carbon dioxide in Earth's atmosphere at the Mauna Loa Observatory. Without a sound study, we could not have proceeded any further.

In 1979, the National Academy of Sciences published a report in the United States titled "Carbon Dioxide and Climate: A Scientific Assessment." That is when the potential of climate warming became the study and research topic. However, the connection between carbon dioxide and the greenhouse effect, a critical factor in climate change, was established a little later.

The greenhouse effect is a process that occurs when gases in Earth's atmosphere trap the Sun's heat. This process makes Earth much warmer than it would be without an atmosphere. The greenhouse effect is one of the things that makes Earth a comfortable place to live. French mathematician Joseph Fourier is credited as the first person to coin the term greenhouse effect based on his conclusion in 1824 that Earth's atmosphere functioned similarly to a "hot box."

It is time to explain the "hotbox ."If parked under the Sun with windows closed on a hot summer day, we all know that our car gets unbearably hot inside because the Sun's energy penetrates the car windows, but the heat has no way of escaping back out. We are making a "hotbox" out of our car! Our Earth works similarly. Sunlight comes through our atmosphere and reaches the surface, transforming into heat. Typically, some heat would escape back into space, but greenhouse gases trap a portion, just like the closed car windows. These gases, including carbon dioxide, act like a blanket completely around Earth, keeping it warm enough to support life. But if we let this blanket get too thick, it will trap too much heat, and the climate will not be comfortable. We humans make this blanket pretty thick, sometimes knowingly, other times due to our comfortable lifestyle. That's the greenhouse effect, and it's not all that mysterious!

By adding more carbon dioxide, forgetting the other gases for now, to the atmosphere, we are supercharging the natural greenhouse effect, causing global temperature to rise. But it is not only carbon dioxide. All the greenhouse gases are the culprits. But carbon dioxide is easy to understand. We cannot breathe in carbon dioxide. So, while the science behind climate change can be intricate, the concept is something we encounter daily. When we hear about reducing our carbon footprint, it simply means slowing down the thickening of that 'blanket.' It's about using energy more efficiently, using renewable energy sources, reducing waste, and making more sustainable choices.

So, I hope I have demystified climate change without citing all the history of the research and technical papers, which may make another book or complicate the understanding. For example, search for "Keeling Curve" to know more if you are interested.

* * *

Addressing the challenge of incorporating visuals,

such as pictures and proper educational websites, into high school and general school social science textbooks is a complex task. We need strong collaboration from Educational platforms to integrate textbooks with reliable, standard, and stable internet networks. Modernizing educational materials at the high school level is problematic. This topic is beyond the scope of this book!

References

NASA provides the robust scientific data needed to understand climate change. Search for NASA, ATTOM, and IPCC.

The Intergovernmental Panel on Climate Change (IPCC) is the leading international body for assessing climate change.

Chapter 1

These days, climate change is a topic that comes up due to the observable trend of above-average temperatures, resulting in warmer climates across the globe. Climate change refers to noticeable

Prologue

deteriorating change in both global and regional climate patterns, which often prove to be unpredictable in nature. Climate Change is primarily driven by the increased release of greenhouse gases, and air pollutants into the atmosphere. Notably, one of the primary contributors to these greenhouse gases is carbon dioxide.

We can quantify the extent of changes in our atmosphere when comparing it to pre-industrial eras and within the last century. Consequently, we now face the pressing challenge of mitigating air pollution and an attempt to reverse the temperature rise, ideally limiting it to 1.5 degrees Celsius.

We all need to think about Climate change

and its implications actively. Global Temperature rise, melting polar ice and glaciers, Sea-level rise, Extreme weather events like incessant rain and wildfires, ocean acidification, and Ecosystem Degradation are some phenomena connected to climate change. Suppose we pollute air beyond the capacity of forests and green trees to clean it. In that case, we are in trouble, which is as simple as that! Awareness, education, action, and behavioral change are crucial to our success. Schools can integrate climate change into their curriculum, and I hope this book will help in that direction.

I am calling this *climate crisis,* hoping everybody, especially the new generation, will find out how to take the atmosphere back to the pre-industrial days. Otherwise, at least a significant part of our Earth may be inhabitable. It is one Eearth, one fragile atmosphere wrapping the world. This layer and our planet require tender, loving care!

I start with the Sun's energy, which makes life possible on Earth and dictates regular climate patterns. The interaction between the Sun and Earth is responsible for the changing seasons, day and night cycles, and various phenomena like solar eclipses when the Moon passes between the Earth and the Sun. How the Earth revolves around the Sun makes climate patterns on the Earth that we take for granted. These are predictable changes, and astronomers and astrophysicists study them. On the other hand, climate change is a challenge and is destructive!

"Jet streams" are included to show ongoing research on higher atmospheres and global air currents. After "Jet Streams" the topics are more or less independent.

Think about an HVAC system installed in a residence or building for heating, ventilation, and air conditioning. When there are variations in occupancy or when the air becomes contaminated by smoke, we can adjust the systems outside air intake. This adjustment is made with other alterations to enhance comfort while considering the system's efficiency. How do we clean Earth's air when it is polluted, mainly due to increased carbon dioxide? Adding more fresh air is not an easy, feasible solution. First, will you get good air from other celestial bodies like the Moon, Mars, or Venus? It highlights the challenge of cleaning Earth's polluted air and emphasizes the realization of it. We cannot underscore the importance of addressing pollution and improving air quality on our planet through more practical means, such as reducing emissions and implementing environmental conservation measures.

Humans and carbon dioxide emissions are problematic; there is no fresh air to add from outside! Our air is a sustainable system cleaned by itself, depending on the green plants and other complicated processes. Without lush forests, the Earth cannot clean up pollution well enough —nature's recycling process is breaking down. It is as simple as that. Please note that Earth's air is connected! What is happening in Timbuctoo is also happening in Kathmandu, immediately or sooner or later!

Let us shift our focus from depleting Earth's resources to revitalizing the planet through sustainable practices such as companion planting, exemplified by methods like the three sisters. By conserving resources today, we are safeguarding the Earth for future generations.

Planting Corn, Squash and beans together
Three sisters wikipedia

The Three Sisters:

The trio of Corn, Squash, and Beans are not just a quaint arrangement in a garden; they represent a profound ecological partnership practiced by indigenous folks for time immemorial. In this agricultural approach, cultivated together, the trio and their symbiotic relationships offer multiple advantages. The concept embodies a form of companion planting where these three crops support each other. Corn provides a natural trellis for the Beans to climb. Beans fix nitrogen in the soil, benefiting Corn, and Squash acts as a living mulch, shading the soil and preventing weeds. Together, they create a harmonious ecosystem that mimics the diversity and cooperation found in natural ecosystems.

One of the key benefits of this method is its potential to deter pests naturally. The principle is simple: different insects have varying preferences for plants. Inter-planting the Three Sisters reduces the likelihood of a single pest infesting all three crops. This diversity acts as a natural pest control mechanism, reducing the need for harmful chemical pesticides.

Robin Wall Kimmerer, the botanist, author, and decorated professor, brought this idea from indigenous wisdom to us in writing. By harnessing the power of natural partnerships and ecological understanding, we can take steps toward restoring the delicate balance between human agriculture and the natural world. A desire for a more harmonious relationship between humans and nature, a belief that we can coexist with the environment in a way that benefits both parties and contributes to the overall well-being of our planet, needs to be fostered to see our nature rebound. We all need to change our mindset. I hope for a rebound of nature. I hope that as you read the book, you'll appreciate the perspective of the harmony of the three sisters. We can research and extend companion planting on a large scale.

Laurence C. Smith is an author known for his work on environmental issues and climate change, particularly related to the Arctic region. Laurence Smith had a chapter titled "California Browning, Shanghai drowning" published two decades ago. How true he has been!

References:

Kimmerer, Robin Wall, "Braiding SweetGrass : Indigenous Wisdom, Scientific Knowledge and the Teachings of Plants", Milkweed Editions, 2013.

Smith, Lawrence C., "The World in 2050", Penguins Group, A Plume Book, USA.

Chapter 2

Our Earth moves around the Sun. The Sun's energy changes the weather and provides the warmth that keeps us alive. Life can only exist on Earth because we receive the required energy from the Sun.

Energy Water and air are the other necessities to sustain life. In general, the Earth and the Sun energy system is predictable and occurs annually, leading to the familiar cycles of spring, summer, fall, and winter. Typical climatic changes are different than the present climate change, and we first need to know the regular system, at least a little. Earth is a self-sustaining system, it cleans its own air and recycles water in the form of water vapor and rain and aligns environmental variables while keeping the ecosystem in sensitive balance. Nature's balance should not be disturbed to the extent where it cannot bounce back easily.

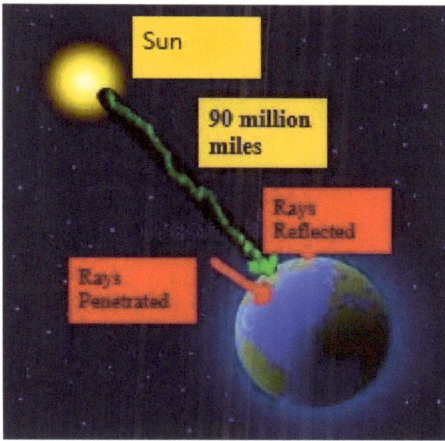

The Sun is Earth's source of energy

As the Earth moves around the Sun, it also rotates on its axis, which causes day and night. We face the Sun during the day but do not at night. The seasons of spring, summer, fall, and winter happen because of how we receive the Sun's power in a particular location and the tilt of the planet's axis. As we progress in our orbit, we get closer and farther away from the Sun, moving from summer to winter.

Some of the Sun's energy penetrates the Earth, and some is reflected into space.

How the energy moves around the planet—through air, land, water, and ice—creates the Earth's weather patterns and climate. These are our typical seasonal changes that have nothing to do with climate change.

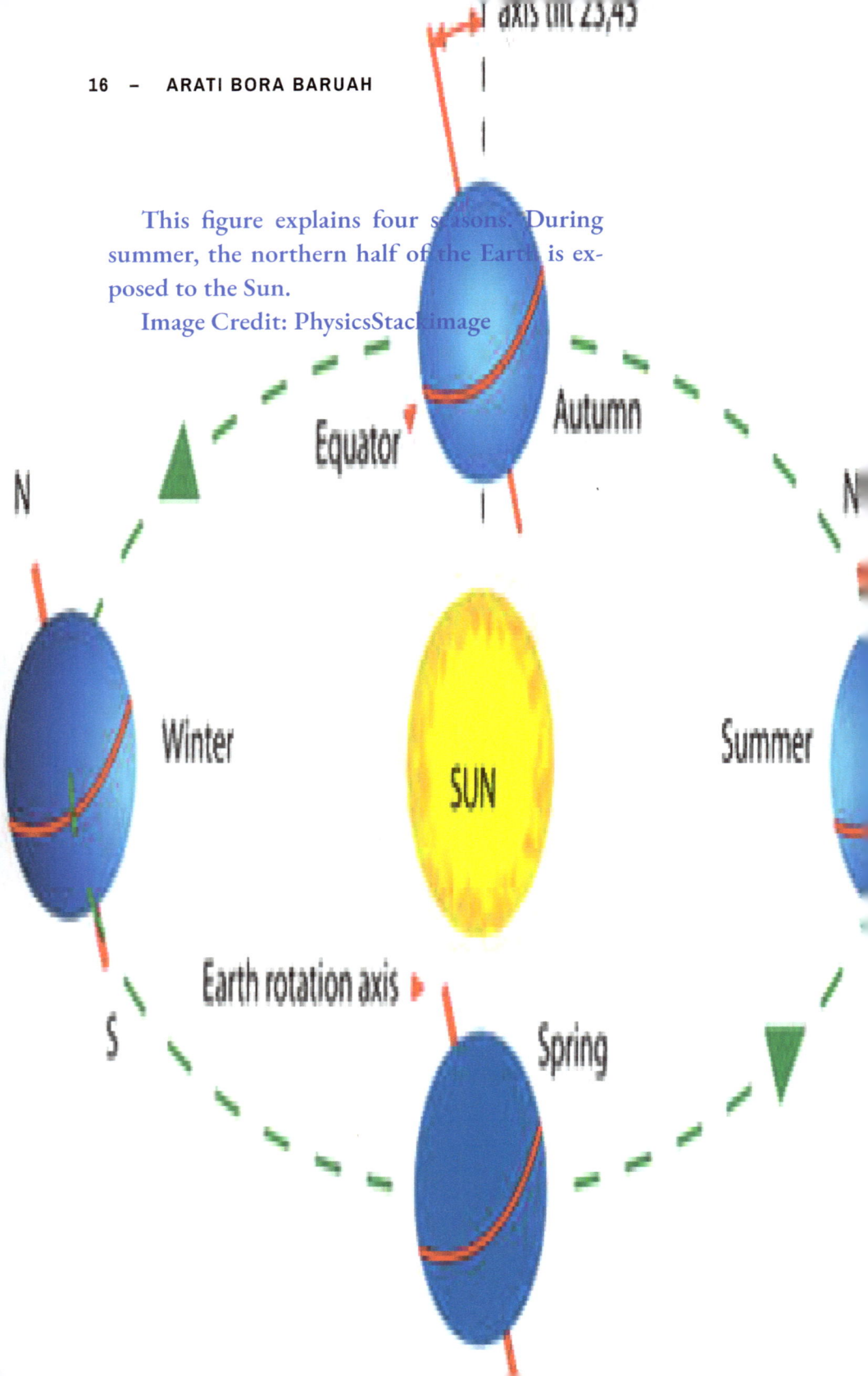

This figure explains four seasons. During summer, the northern half of the Earth is exposed to the Sun.

Image Credit: PhysicsStackimage

Some other periodic changes happen to our planet because of the properties of Earth itself.

Scientists have noted three changes listed below, all of which happen over thousands of years. These changes are periodic but with a long period of time. We mention them here to not to confuse them with climate change.

1. Change in the tilt of Earth's axis,
2. Change of eccentricity of Earth's oval orbit, and
3. Precession.

Eccentricity is when the oval orbit almost becomes circular. Precession refers to how Earth's orbit moves around the Sun, like a hula hoop swings around your waist. All these are natural processes that happen because of small variations of Earth's spinning and orbiting. Changes happen depending on which side of Earth gets more energy. These changes are natural, and astronomers and scientists can monitor them and alert us on the status of Earth's orbit. This means we know when natural changes are coming and can prepare for them. This allows astronomers to do their work and predict the difference in climate, but it is not related to present climate change. We expect planetary changes affect earth's climate, but we need to distinguish known ones with from climate changes which are human human-made and we really do not understand what we are doing to ourselves, I mean to eEarth itself.

However, it has been seen in certain cases that the tilt of Earth's axis may have changed because of human-made causes. This is quite complex, and more research and investigation are required. One example could be the construction of a giant dam. The weight of water can change the center of gravity and tilt of Earth. Solar flares are sudden bursts of energy from the Sun and are magnetic in nature. Solar flares do happen and affect electrical distribution. We leave these out of the climate change process.

References

Scientific American Article, "We Live in the Rearest Type of Planetary System", Lee Billings, 2023. (scientificamerican.com)

Planetary Systems, Planetary-Science.org

Planets - NASA Science (.gov)

https://science.nasa.gov/solar-system/planets/

Chapter 3

The air we breathe is part of a thin layer of roughly five miles (eight kilometers) called the Atmospheric Layer. This layer wraps around the planet and shields us from dangerous radiation

Atmosphere, Pollution and Storms

from space. The Earth's atmosphere comprises about 78 percent nitrogen, 21 percent oxygen, and 1 percent other gases. The clouds we see in the sky, the wind that moves the leaves on the trees and makes waves on a rice field, and the Sunshine we feel on our faces are all because of the Earth's atmosphere.

Pollution is a much broader term encompassing various harmful substances released into the environment, including air, water, soil, and noise pollution. Pollution can come from multiple sources, including industrial processes, transportation, agriculture, and improper waste disposal are a few examples. Pollution is very harmful to our bodies and contributes to climate change to some extent.

Carbon dioxide (CO2) makes up only about 0.04 percent of the atmosphere today, but the weird fact is that Earth's atmospheric CO2 has increased 50 percent since the industrial revolution. It has not been this high in millions of years. As we know humans exhale carbon dioxide and cannot live with excess of it. Uunless we perfected carbon capture, humans are in trouble.

Here is where our story starts, the climate change crisis! Let us repeat it again!
Carbon dioxide has not been this high in millions of years.

The Sun, Earth, Earth's atmosphere, and pollution. The culprits of greenhouse gas emissions are our day-to-day friends, cars, homes, industries, trucks, animal farms, and wildfires!

While the atmosphere is vast compared to the human scale, it is a finite resource, and its ability to absorb pollutants and regulate climate has limits. Earth's atmosphere is also an interconnected system that envelops planet Earth. The atmosphere provides crucial roles, including providing oxygen for respiration, regulating the Earth's temperature by trapping heat through the greenhouse effect, protecting the Earth's surface from harmful solar radiation, and supporting weather patterns and climate.

The atmosphere is constantly in motion because of Earth's rotation and temperature differences. This circulation results in weather patterns, wind, and ocean climates influencing global climate.

Interconnectedness: The atmosphere is a dynamic system where changes in one part can affect the other. The interconnectedness highlights the need for global cooperation to address environmental issues. Conservation and sustainable practices are essential to protect this vital system.

References

"Atmosphere, The: An Introduction to Meteorology", by Frederick K Lutgens (Author), Edward J. Tarbuck (Author), Redina Herman (Author), Dennis G. Tasa (illustrator), Pearson, 2018

Chapter 4

Typically, the climate pattern of Earth is relatively stable, even though the Earth goes through warmer and cooler periods. In the

Climate Patterns

United States and Europe, we expect to have a few 90°-degree-Fahrenheit (32° degrees Centigrade) days during the summer and a few happy snowy months in the winter. But these expectations may soon no longer be the norm.

Changes in the climate are caused by human-made activities. If the balance of carbon dioxide in the air increases, the Earth's average temperature will also rise—which has already happened!

Humans and animals breathe in oxygen and breathe out CO2, while plants do the opposite. We need plants to keep us alive, but in recent decades, we have cut down many, many trees and cleared away many, many forests. Cutting down forests is a significant reason for climate change. Burning fossil fuels—which increased drastically with the Industrial Revolution—also releases CO2.

Extreme hot and cold days, wildfires, and extreme rains causing flash floods are all becoming increasingly common due to climate change. Have you heard these names for hurricanes: Katrina, Ivan, and Maria? Intense storms like those are caused by climate change.

The USA has varied climates. California, Alabama, Arizona, Texas, Florida, Georgia, Mississippi, Louisiana, the Carolinas, Arkansas, and Hawaii are considered warm states. Out of fifty states, Northern Arizona and New Mexico, central and northern Nevada, and most of Utah have a semi-desert climate but colder and snowier winters. It is possible to have a hurricane (the other name is cyclone), a tropical phenomenon, and a blizzard simultaneously in different parts of the country.

El Niño (or El Nino) and La Niña refer to two parts of an extreme weather pattern that returns every two or three years. It occurs in the Pacific region between Australia and the Americas. As early as 1600, South American fishermen noticed unusually warm water occurring in the Pacific Ocean in a regular cycle and named it El Niño (meaning "little boy" in Spanish). They grew to expect poor fishing during this time. El Niño can also refer to Jesus Christ, which was fitting, as El Niño often occurred during Christmast.

During El Niño, winds cause warm surface water to move east, toward Central and South America. However, El Niño can be quite big and even affect the whole world. The basic principle to take away from this is that temperature increases in the air can, in turn, cause an increase in the ocean temperature, which can cause storms that can affect the entire planet. Change in temperature is a key issue. El Niño has caused drought in certain countries.

La Niña is simply a cold event during which trade winds are even stronger than usual, pushing more warm water toward Asia. If these events become more powerful—which they will, with a warming climate—the negative effects will increase dramatically as well. In the North and Central aAmerican region we are aware of these changes and predict weather effects of these events.

References

Internet search on National Weather Service (NWS), a branch of the National Oceanic and Atmospheric Administration (NOAA)

NOAA/NWS Storm Prediction Center, also search for Storm Prediction Center (SPC) (.gov)

https://www.spc.noaa.gov

Henson Robert, "The Rough Guide to Climate Change, the Symptoms, the Science, the Solutions", 3rd Edition, Rough Guides Ltd, 2011

www.martin.fl.us/about-hurricanes

Next Page: Eye-of-a-storm (hurricane, cyclone, or typhoon) is the calm or stable part of a storm and is crucial to identify practical aspects so that emergency responses can be prompt and disaster recovery can be done.

Chapter 5

The glass walls of a greenhouse trap gases like CO2, nitrous oxide (NO), methane (CH4), Water Vapor, and ozone (03). Together these gasses are called greenhouse gases.

The Greenhouse Effect

Doing so keeps the plants inside warmer, year-round, just like a car with windows closed can get very hot in the Sun. As mentioned earlier Earth's atmosphere reflects some of the incoming radiation and absorbs and recycles the rest. Gasses that absorb longwave radiation are the greenhouse gases. Most of the time I leave water vapor out of greenhouse gases because unlike Carbon dioxide it recycles easy, The Moon neither has an atmosphere nor greenhouse effect, and we can learn a lot by comparing "air-less" Moon to our Earth!

The Greenhouse gases have a similar warming effect on the Earth's atmosphere if they are in high quantities—and their quantities in our atmosphere are increasing over time, because of human involvement in climate change. This is called the greenhouse effect. So the process of heating by greenhouse gases is the Greenhouse Effect.

Permafrost generally refers to the mud beneath the arctic tundra that stays permanently frozen. Siberia and Tibet contain permafrost,wh ich emits trapped methane ($CH4$) when it heats up and melts. Oil and gas wells and landfills also release methane. Cattle and sheep belch up methane, too. Greenhouse gases can be released in ways we may not even expect. Dams, for example, create water reservoirs that release plenty of methane in tropical and subtropical places, because they drown plants and animals, which rot and expel methane.

Ozone (03), when in the right amount, protects us from the Sun's harmful ultraviolet rays. There is a thin layer of ozone on top of the atmosphere.

Next Page

Quick Pictionary demonstrates the maximum and minimum temperature humans can tolerate without heat stroke and freezing. They are shown in both Fahrenheit and Celsius scales. The Fahrenheit scale is pretty much designed to reflect the range of the human tolerance scale. The Celsius equivalents are offered too.

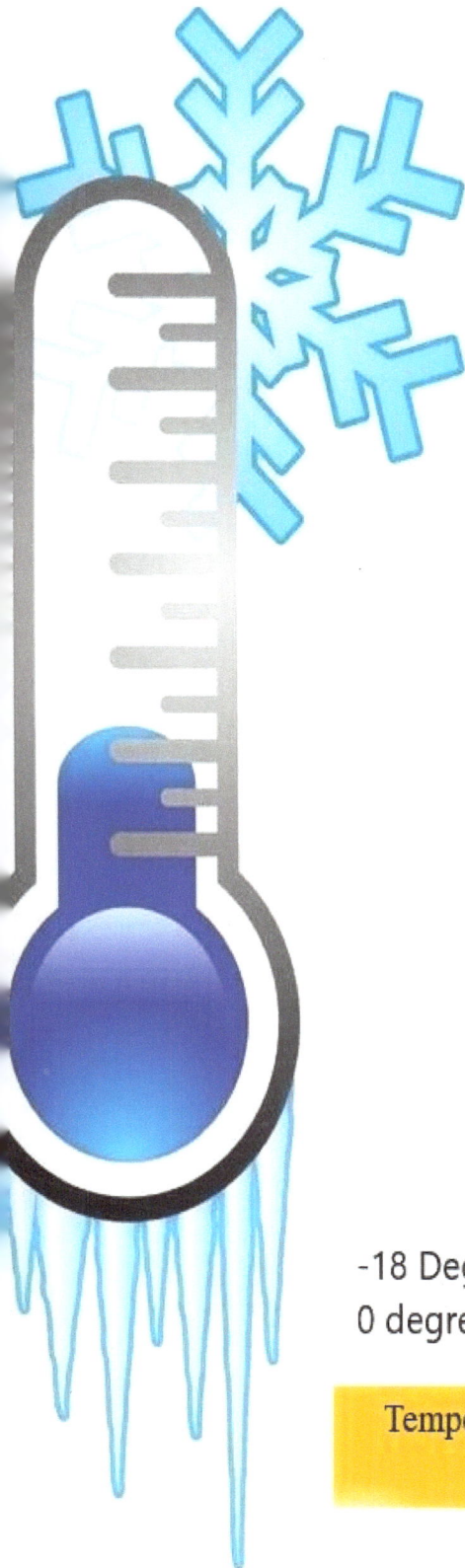

-18 Degree C
0 degree F

42 Degree C
108 Degree F

Temperature range that a human body can withstand

Diverse weather—a few rainy days and some sunny days—are what we like. Severe storms and blizzards are some of the weather's angry sides, but even they should naturally occur now and then. Different regions have a particular pattern. Some are very dry, some are cool, and some are wet—but whatever they are, over a hundred years, this pattern can change. While we like weather patterns to be consistent, this may not happen.

Weather patterns can change naturally, but human involvement can speed up these changes much more quickly and drastically than we would like.

We have released a lot of greenhouse gases, which have warmed the planet, which has melted permafrost, which has released even more greenhouse gases. This is causing extreme hot weather, which is causing catastrophic wildfires, which is wiping out plants that could have helped mitigate the greenhouse gas issue. Excessive rains have caused the ground to soak up so much moisture that the land is eroding, and trees are uprooting!

This is causing warmer weather, yes, but also so much more. Growing food requires a stable weather pattern; unexpected floods and drought will diminish food production, and farmers' worries will soon become everyone's issues.

The oceans—Pacific, Atlantic, Indian, Southern, and Arctic—soak up the Sun's rays and drive the weather patterns worldwide. Oceans can hold more heat than any other body, such as grasslands. The oceans have more CO2 than anything else on Earth, —nature's carbon capture utility!

Ocean water is salty, and we can only drink fresh water. Rivers and glaciers have fresh water. As a river flows through the land, it brings salt and other minerals to the ocean, making the water salty.

Only 3 Percent of the world's water is fresh drinkable water.

This is important to realize. Even some of the lakes have salty water. Ocean and sea water is salty. Desalination is an expensive operation. Additionally, we cannot dump salt from the plant anywhere expect for beaches because most of the plants won't grow in salty water.

References
NOAA/NWS Storm Prediction Center
Storm Prediction Center (.gov)
https://www.spc.noaa.gov

Chapter 6

Jet streams are the air currents driven by the differences between cooler and higher temperatures.   Cooler temperatures are primarily due to oceans and

Jet Streams

the poles. Different ground levels make different layers of hot or hotter air currents. We need to know about jet stream because it also drives weather patterns.

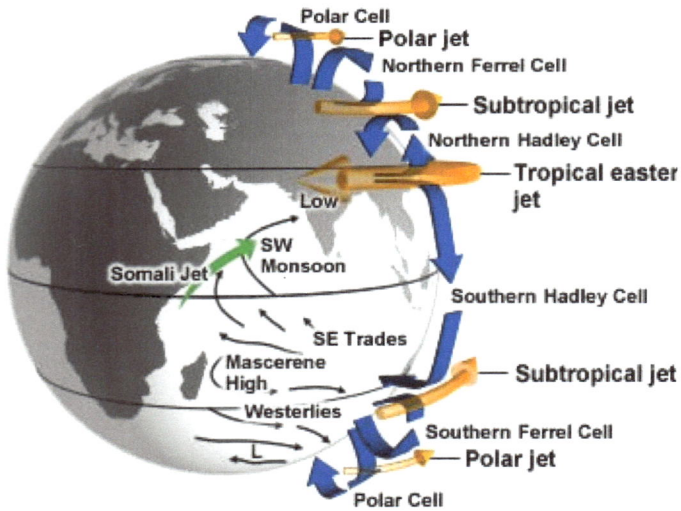

NCAR/The COMET Program

The figure above shows how jet streams move around. Monsoon dynamics are also shown.

Understanding the relationship between jet stream patterns and climate change is crucial in mitigating the impacts of climate change. Research on this issue barely evolves, and scientists are trying to understand atmospheric dynamics. The air masses that cover large, significant geographical areas significantly impact weather patterns as they move around the globe. When we say the Earth moves around the Sun, we talk about one Earth, disregarding its geophysical boundaries. Models of Earth's atmosphere when it moves globally are not working well yet. When jet stream patterns meander around, it can cause shifts in weather patterns.

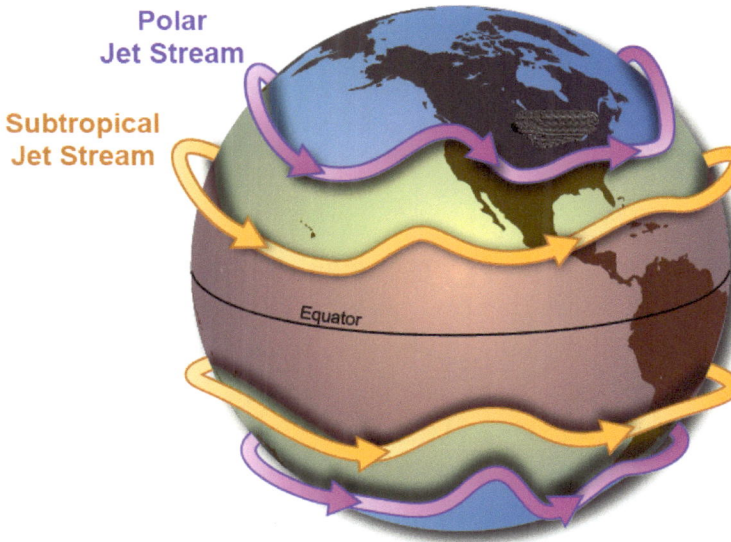

Polar Jet Stream
Subtropical Jet Stream
Equator

Jet streams occur in both hemispheres. The 50°–60° latitude north and south regions are where the polar jets are located, and around 30° north and south are where the subtropical jet streams are found. The name "jet streams" comes from the fact that jet airplanes cruise within the jet streams. The picture is at the end of this chapter. That's why we get a headwind in the US while flying from California to New York and a tailwind on the return trip—in other words, that's why it's faster to fly east than west across the US.

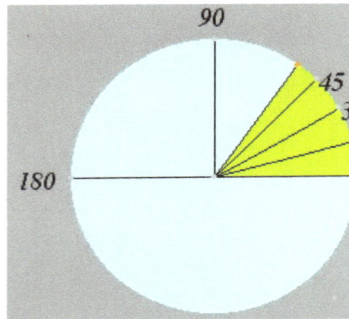

polar angle is 90 degrees at the north pole

Subtropical jet streams play some role on the Asian side because of the high Himalayan range. The freezing wind poses a significant danger to the climbers on Mount Everest because of the subtropical jet stream. The subtropical jet wind divides into two branches by the Himalayan and Tibetan plateau and meets up again off the east coast of China. Subtropical jet streams may affect the timing of Indian monsoons. These studies are very new and show how the layers of air move high in the sky. (We need you to find this topic interesting to follow up on when you grow up.) Jet streams will help predict more on how pollution on one part of Earth moves to other regions.

Interestingly, the subtropical jet streams on the Eurasian side of the globe are just above the highest mountains and the highest part of the world. All over the world, most of the mountain ranges are north and south—except for the Eurasian side. Starting with the high country of Tajikistan, Pamirs, Hindukush, Karakoram, and the thousands of miles-long Himalayas are lined up with jet streams. It has quite an effect on the world's atmosphere—and that's not even counting the monsoon; it has not been exhaustively studied yet!

The subtropical jet stream and the monsoon are vital in stabilizing the climate. From my research, I call the mountain region of central Asia and Tibet Autonomous Region- the Vertical Pole. As mentioned earlier, the subtropical jet stream sometimes splits in the Himalayan area and then meets again in the South China Sea. However, its role and relationship with monsoon winds are not entirely understood.

Mountains and oceans are the controllers of overall global air movements. The air above the Earth is globally connected. The effect of the mountains can be realized if we imagine five-mile-high and over thousand-mile-long Himalayan mountain ranges replacing the Great Lakes of the US and Canada. Please consult the pictures provided. It would drastically change the climate of the US and Canada. For instance, the US has great lakes in its north. The mid-American region becomes very cold when cold air comes further down from Canada. It happens when the polar jet dips further down. Suppose there was a grand barrier, a wall, or tall mountains in the north of the US instead of the lakes. The climate of the US would have been drastically different. We will revisit this topic later. The primary purpose of it is to explain how humans can alter nature without thinking. It helps us to be informed about what role mountains play in the weather.

Oceanic Circulation definitely can influence weather from

local to global. Jet Streams are example of global circulation. Subtropical jet streams is more of a winter time jet and is weaker than the polar jet stream.

References

NCAR - The National Center for Atmospheric Research (NCAR) Mesa Lab sits nestled against the foothills to the Rocky Mountains in Boulder.

Also see references for the chapter on "Atmosphere, Pollution and Storms".

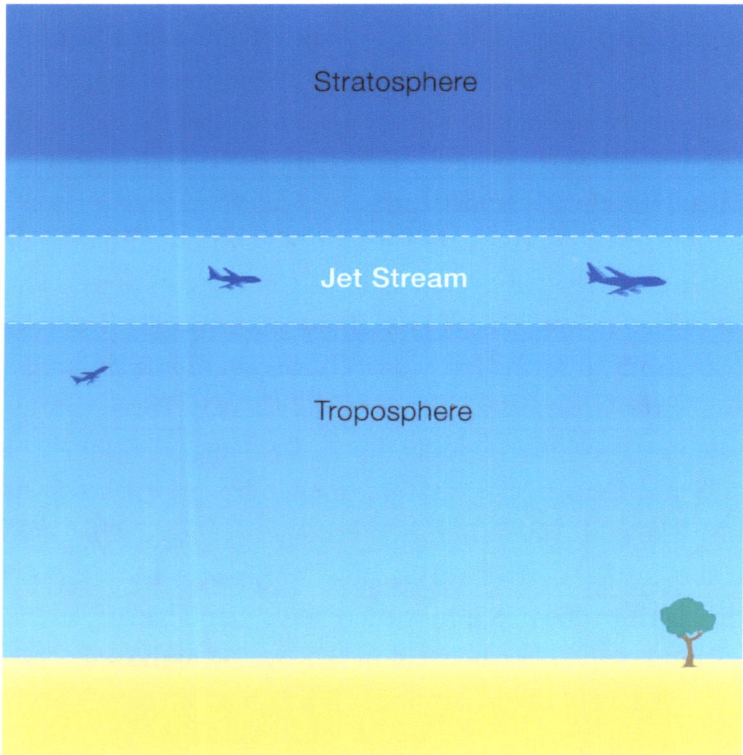

Stratosphere and Troposphere Layers

Chapter 7

Glaciers are huge chunks of moving ice in the Earth's polar regions and high mountains. Glaciers grow in the winter and melt in summer.

Glaciers

When the median heat of the world increases, the glaciers may melt faster. This is especially true since temperature rise happens six times faster near the poles than near the equator. In the North and South Poles, vast chunks of glaciers are breaking up and melting!

Melting ice causes the sea level to rise and inundate the coastal lands, which is happening now! Glacier melting is drowning some coastal places worldwide. Jakarta, the capital of Indonesia, will likely be submerged by 2050 because of rising sea water and sinking land. Bangladesh, a country in Asia, is especially vulnerable because of its topography. The National Oceanic and Atmospheric Administration has made sea level rise viewers available in the US. Relocation of several coastal regions has already had to happen in the US, and even more will happen soon.

Reference:

Search for "how much is the Antartica Icesheet melting?"

Melting Glaciers

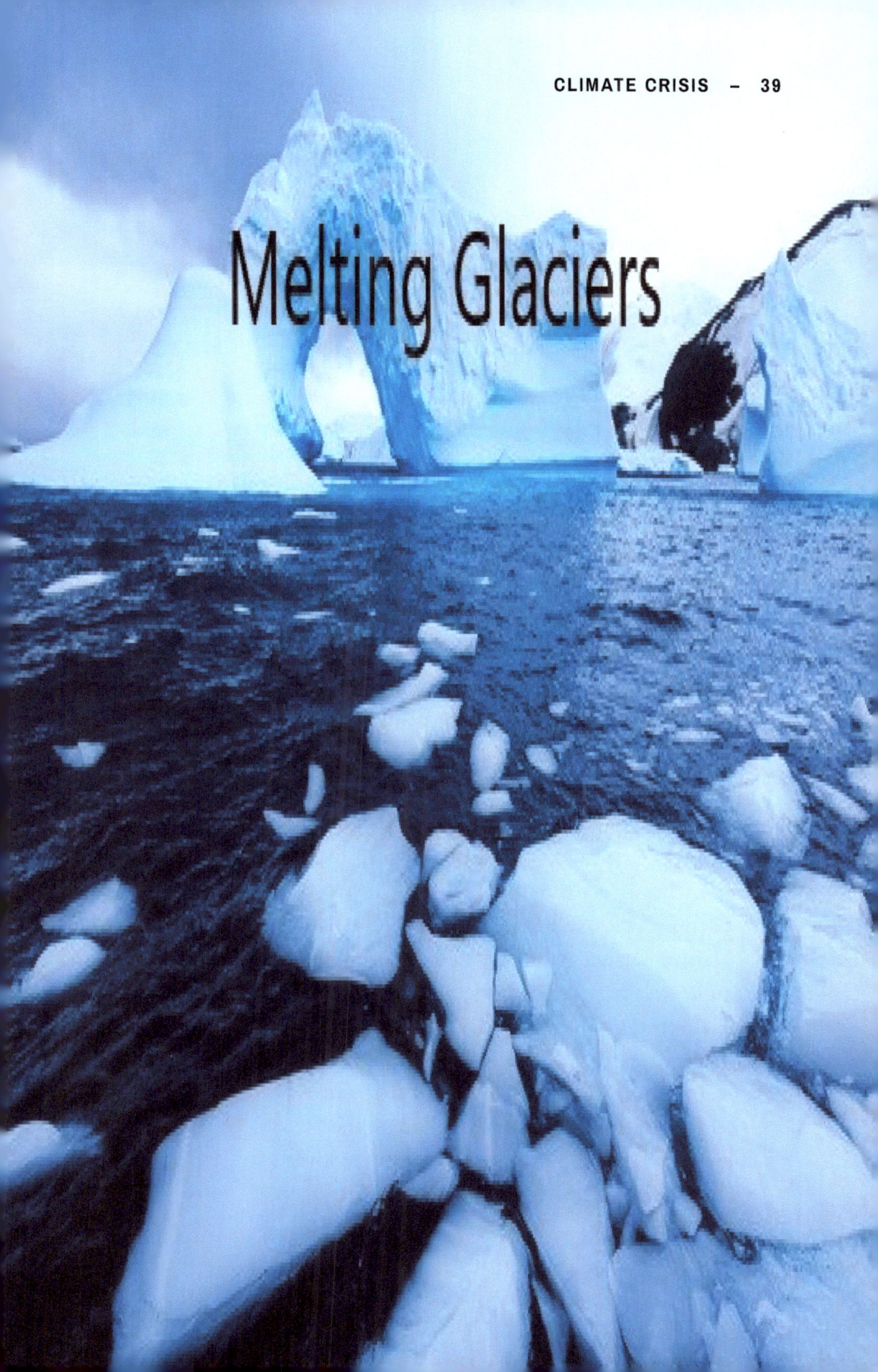

Chapter 8

Remote sensing satellites track weather around the Earth by collecting weather data. The satellites offer a bird's-eye view of the Earth's weather pat-

Tracking Cyclical Processes

terns. Satellites can document smog, sea ice, melting glaciers, and deforestation worldwide by comparing data over time. Land and mountain weather stations also have instruments for measuring atmospheric data. Together, they can forecast bad weather and warn us. Weather is just one of Earth's natural cycles.

Nature balances several cyclical processes—including weather, the carbon cycle, and the eco-cycle—in order to keep our air clean by balancing oxygen and carbon dioxide. We know plants do not eat food by mouth like us, but use the process called "photosynthesis." In this process, the green "chlorophyll" part of the plant's leaves converts carbon dioxide from the Sun's rays into oxygen, like how we breathe in oxygen and breathe out carbon dioxide. The plant's process requires Sunlight, water, and carbon dioxide. From there, animals and humans get a lot of food and nutrition. Birds and bees pollinate the flowers, spread the plants, and new growth happens.

Clouds also have a cycle. Formed by evaporated water vapor, they move up to the sky and come back as rain to Earth. When the water content of the clouds increases so that the clouds cannot hold it anymore, rain happens. When it rains, small particles and pollutants in the air come down with the rain, cleaning the air. Rain is also needed for plants to grow. Everything is connected by these processes. The "kid's picture" on the next page is an attempt to explain clouds, photosynthesis and spreading of seeds by birds and animals.

Weather patterns, land and ocean winds, ocean currents, and continuous rain are all made by a worldwide natural process. Deserts, oceans, the Himalayas, and the Amazon rainforests all work together in a complicated process that does not follow geographical boundaries. To have the ultimate balance in nature, we need all plants and animals, predators and prey, and even parasites working together.

However, nature has a limit, and we humans currently hamper some of the processes. This balance is very delicate and requires all-hands-on-deck to repair.! Working toward protecting it means all the world to you and me—literally.! If kids and youths today can learn these processes, they can grow to live in harmony with nature.

References

"Make a Water Cycle Model", Science Sparks website.

Next Page
The kid's picture:
Get kids involved in understanding the role of nature

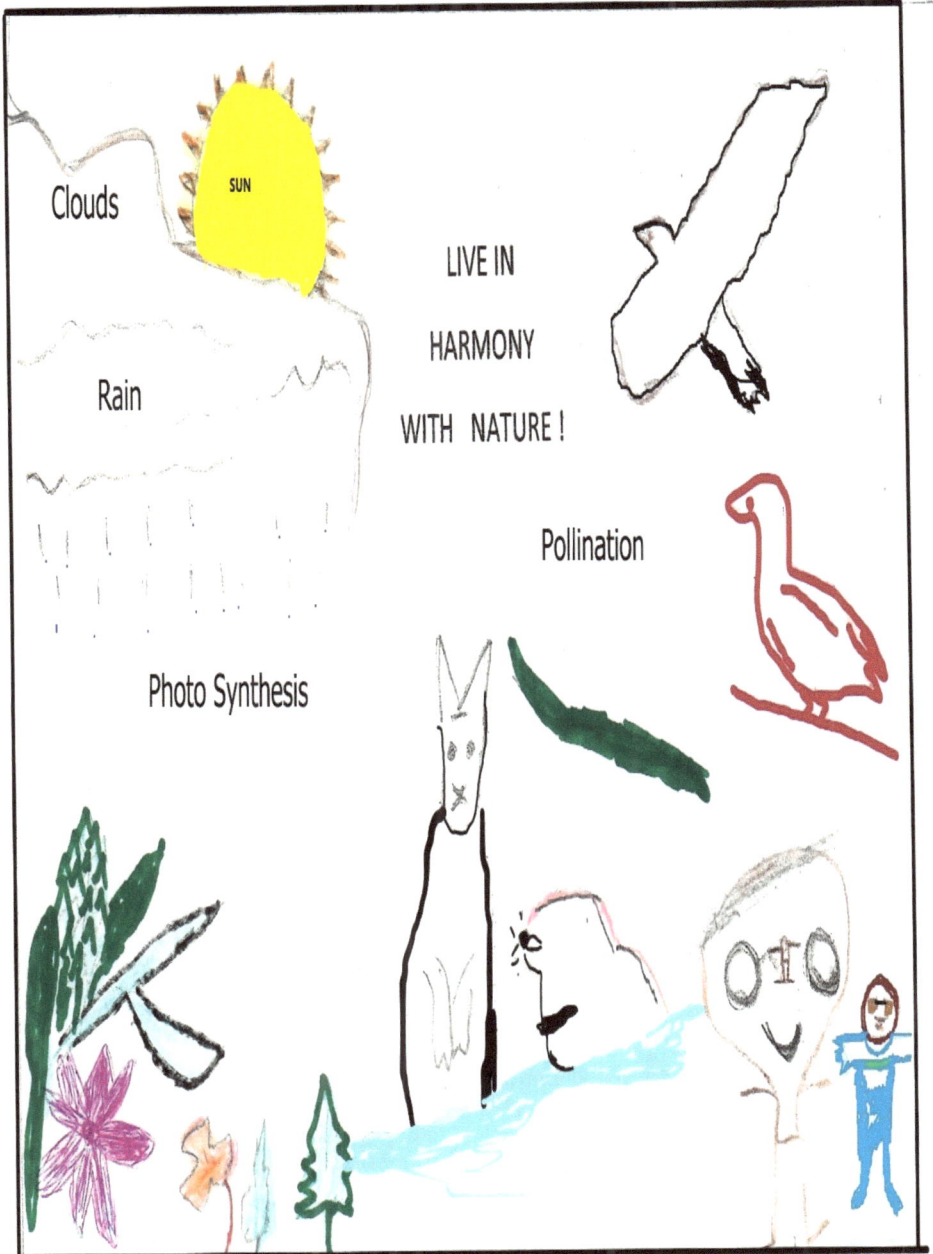

Chapter 9

Recycle, Reuse, Support Renewable Energy, Carbon Capture, Go Green, and Save Nature. We all are doing some recycling—mainly, we recycle paper, cardboard, and paper-based packag-

What can we do?

ing. Recycled materials are reused to make other needed products. Look for the sign that says, "Made with recycled products" and try to support companies that do so.

However, recycling is only part of the solution. Fossil fuels, like coal and petroleum, are energy sources that run our cars, heat our homes, and cook our food, and when they burn, they release CO_2. We extract these products from the Eearth by mining. Once ignited, they are gone—forever. They are not renewable. They pollute, and they are limited. That's why we need to be talking about renewable energy sources that do not pollute.

Electric cars have much smaller carbon footprints (meaning, they use far fewer nonrenewable resources and pollute far less), and the lithium batteries they run on can be recycled and reused. But they aren't a perfect solution; we still need to charge the battery, and that electric source needs to be fossil-fuel–free, too. While there is plenty of lithium in the world, lithium also must be mined. It comes mixed up with other materials, like copper, gold, aluminum, and diamond. Extracting the lithium from these other materials is a complicated process that must be green as well. "Going green" means that the process is environmentally friendly and does not produce harmful pollutants. At the moment, most lithium mining is not green. If untreated industrial waste from lithium extraction reaches water, that water will be undrinkable.

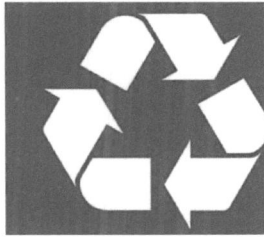

Carbon capture is a process in which a relatively pure stream of carbon dioxide from industrial sources is separated, treated, and transported to a long-term storage location. Carbon capture is expensive, but in the future we will have to do it in every factory.

Chapter 10

The most awkward, troubling, uncomfortable, and sometimes disagreeable aspect of climate change is that the cause is activities done by humans. Even though technology provides an immensely positive impact on our day-to-day lives, it has side ef-

Human Activities

fects. All power plants cause harmful emissions. We already know that deforestation, overpopulation, transportation (burning fossil fuel), landfills, fertilizers, and garbage deposits are on the list of human activities that negatively impact the increasing carbon footprint, but the truth is that nearly everything—even agriculture—is on this list. The big farms contribute to waste products of methane and carbon dioxide.

As a species, we cannot just focus on being more productive and raising our standard of living without considering the consequences. We must educate ourselves and contribute to striking the delicate balance our planet needs. Some technologies, such as engineering rivers and building mega-dams for producing electricity in inappropriate environments, need reevaluation. Nuclear power, used as an energy producer, must be examined closely; it is greener than other options but is a complex trade-off, knowing the potential destructive radiation fallout.

Overusing nature's bounty has not been done to this extent before, but the concept is nothing new. We probably caused some prominent river civilizations to die out in the past by taking advantage of nature. History can tell a lot about rivers changing courses and valleys becoming deserts.

Malta's temple people had a vibrant culture and advanced agriculture from 4000 BCE. The question arises: why did it disappear? Studies using soil cores from the Earth's inner layers show that rapid climate change probably caused their demise. There was proof of deforestation. The environment cannot steadily neutralize pollution unless there are extensive forests—and, without forests, food is harder and harder to find.

Today, there is much visual evidence of a warming planet. A retreating and almost dying glacier in Peru at 15,000 feet and above is becoming a tourist museum named "Route to Climate Change." Peruvian Andes and Peru's highlands could once boast the largest concentration of tropical glaciers, but now, these glaciers are shrinking rapidly.

Chapter 11

This Hollywood hill was once full of pumas like the one in the image on the next page. After shrinking of habitat, the "celebrity cat" had to be content with eight square miles, which included two freeways.

Human Impact, Hollywood Cat

This collared puma is a great study of the fate of urbanized animals and how we will have to learn and address the struggle between humans and animals. This example is given to examine what is happening in some parts of the United States. In some parts of the world it is human-elephant concerns. Human-monkey conflict is also reaching a sad stage. Elephants, and rhinoceros are vegetarian animals, their sizes are bigger than carnivores like lions and tigers, but all of them need a bigger area in which to move around. Their grazing areas are shrinking every day.

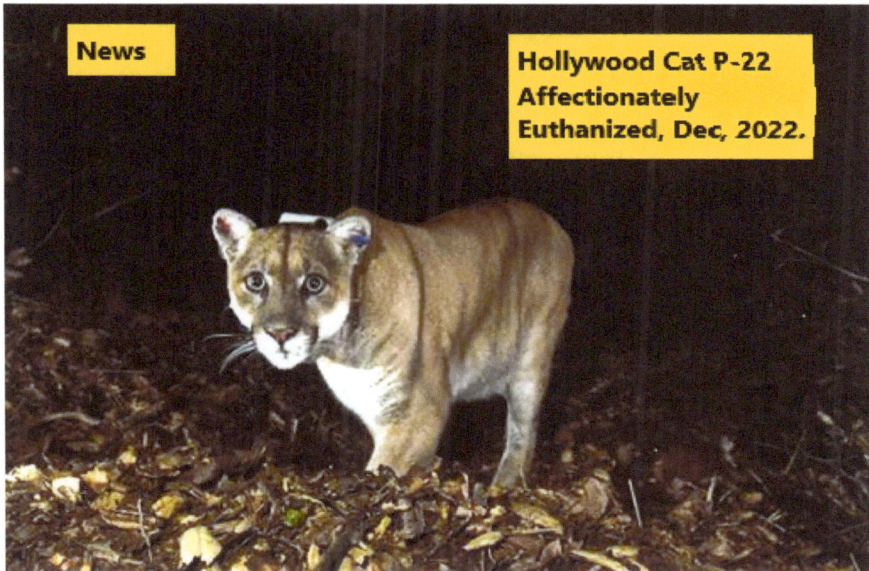

News

Hollywood Cat P-22 Affectionately Euthanized, Dec, 2022.

Chapter 12

Crawford Lake, known as the "bottomless lake" by the natives in Ontario, Canada, holds history within its sediment layers. In the deepest layers, water does not move. The isolated and undisturbed sediments contain a timeline of the recent past. In most lakes, seasonal changes in tempera-

State of the Art Researches at Crawford Lake

ture make water mix from top to bottom. However, in Crawford Lake the deep bottom layer of water never mixes with the top layers. In other words, it preserves history in its sediment layers. The indigenous nations, namely Haudenosaunee (Iroquois), knew about it. This prompted several studies of this lake. One of these obtained a core sample from the bottom of the lake. This deepest layer has cultigens, pollens from the cultivated land species, fly ash, microbes, algae, and even the radionuclides from each summer, just like tree rings.

It is fascinating that plutonium and cesium, bomb-produced radionuclides, were detected from the years 1946–47. That is the time period of World War II, when bomb nuclides got deposited across the globe and on this lake bottom! Just like volcano ashes goes everywhere, pollutants dissipates slowly and eventually go everywhere. Earth's atmosphere is too fragile. As pollutants become widespread, research of wind patterns helps us not only understand the effects of human activity on even the remote corners of Earth, but also how to prevent unwanted catastrophes. That the bomb detonated half a world apart can have particles dissipated all over the world is a reality! Once in the atmosphere, volcanic ash or any other pollutant is subject to prevailing wind patterns. These upper-level winds, which we studies as the jet streams, can carry ash particles across continents and even between hemispheres. The direction and strength of these winds play a crucial role in determining where the ash ultimately settles.

References

"Make a Water Cycle Model", Science Sparks website.

Next Page: For a detailed picture of a clear sectional with annual layers and significant events of Crawford Lake Core, please consult the Anthropocene Working Group website for copyrighted information.

Chapter 13

When we were cavemen, we hunted and gathered for food. As our populations increased, we soon learned that hunting and gathering was not a sustainable model. It took little time to deplete the

Nature's Balancing Act and Nature's Fury

food species in an area. Humans thus started moving from place to place in search of food and eventually discovered agriculture. It is much easier to grow food and raise animals to eat than it is to hunt them down.

Agriculture then changed the face of the Earth. We depleted the natural forests and grasslands as we took more agricultural land. Fast-forward to the present technological era, and you can plainly see that we have changed the world even more. Humankind's interactions with nature need profound studies as we reflect on our actions. Is technological advancement a necessary evil, or is it all good? It is hard to say. Now that we are in the confluence of technology with artificial intelligence (namely generative AI, which can generate alternate versions that could be far from reality), the jury will be out for a while!

Technological advancement aside, it is high time to learn about the harm from mining and extraction of metals, whether they are precious or not. Acids, mercury, and lead may leak out of the ground from these activities. Factories dump pollutants into our waters, resulting in plastics in the stomachs of whales. We need to find solutions to mitigate negative human impact on the world. Plastic wastes are littering the ocean. The Great Pacific Garbage Patch is a gyre of plastic and debris in the north-central Pacific Ocean. It's the largest accumulation of plastic in the world. (Google)

To make a country—and the world—great, green, and sustainable is a challenging goal. Education on this topic reaching everybody early is a partial solution. In that vein, here are some issues that need to be in our perspective. The next three chapters are on these issues.

Chapter 14

The latest average temperature increase on the Earth can significantly increase the population of certain insects, which can go haywire in certain places—locusts and beetles are some examples.

Rewilding

A couple of degrees more can make the wheat production take longer, or not mature at all. We have already lost a large amount number of forests to furniture-making and house-building. Of late, humans have understood the values of trees but have not reconciled to the fact that other ecosystems, such as grasslands, savannah, taiga, steppe, and tundra (permafrost) ecosystems are equally important.

An agrarian culture brought in the domestication of animals, and we are only just beginning to understand the negative impacts of this. At least we have largely stopped using lions and tigers in circuses and learned that carnivores play a big part in a healthy ecosystem. Their preying on herbivores results in a balanced food chain. Without fear of big predators, populations of prey animals can grow wildly, causing nuisance and disease.

Monkeys are a wonderful creation of nature with the high acrobatic skill to live on the jungle canopy without worrying about powerful predators like wolves, tigers, and lions. When they grow in numbers, humans need to find ways to coexist with them. Monkeys are creating real nuisances in certain Asian cities! As humans take over monkeys' habitats, monkeys come to cities in significant gangs. Monkeys enter people's houses, steal food, and ransack office buildings. Now we have animals that are even adapting to big cities.

Urban and suburban animals and their behavior are just becoming research topics, and whispers of "rewilding" are being heard. Rewilding aims at restoring natural ecosystems and habitats, reintroducing native species, and removing human-made structures. In the US, starting in mid-1990, Yellowstone Park reintroduced wolves. The Netherlands has a big project to restore wetland and grassland habitats. Scotland is trying to restore native Caledonian forests, whereas Spain and Portugal are reintroducing Iberian lynx.

In developing countries, if suburbia coexists with a green environment, it can help the birds, bees, and, hopefully, the butterflies. However, studies are needed to check if this encourages more aggressive animals like raccoons and coyotes.

References

Paul Jepson (Author), Cain Blythe (Author), "Rewilding: The radical new science of ecological recovery (Hot Science)", Paperback, MIT Press, September 15, 2020.

Chapter 15

Similarly, a new and healthy perspective has started on dams, mainly mega-dams. The benefits of mega-dams primarily depend on the environment. Mega-dams refer to hydel projects that produce electricity on a mega scale.

Hydel Projects

Dams built on hills with loose, uncompact soils are unstable and erosion-prone. Building massive dams is causing problems in the Himalayan and western regions of China. The Himalayas are the world's youngest mountains, and some hills are erosion-prone.

We are, thankfully, trying to right some of our past wrongs in this area. Many dams were decommissioned in Washington state to let the Salmon move freely to the oceans while spawning. After decades of planning, the most extensive dam removal in US history began in Washington State on September 17, 2011. Six months later, the Elwha Dam was gone, followed by the Glines Canyon Dam in 2014. Today, the Elwha River flows freely from its headwaters in the Olympic Mountains to the Strait of Juan de Fuca.

These are expensive changes but necessary ones. Education is needed to ensure we stop making these mistakes in the first place since it is even harder to correct errors later than not to make them.

Additionally, mega-dam reservoirs, made by filling up green forested hillsides, emit high amounts of methane, causing global warming. The plants and animals die and rot, producing methane, rated the second most important greenhouse gas. Mega-dams for hydroelectricity are justified by saying there will be no further decrease of water downstream once a reservoir is filled up—that is only a tiny part of the equation! Mega-dams are killing ecosystems, causing major flooding by releasing water, dislocating people, and causing erosion. Mega-dams are causing huge lakes of rotten plants and animals and are becoming storage places for sediments and silt.

"I, the author, along with local geologists, geophysicists, river researchers, and the affected communities of Ranga River dam, Subansiri dam, and Uttarakhand hills, present a consensus on mega dams in the Himalaya region. This collective understanding is further elaborated in another book of mine, which is soon to be published."

"I personally welcome small hydroelectric projects but not mega dams. Dams producing more than 100 megawatts do more harm than benefit. This is

a major issue in Asia and Africa now. I have been researching the above issue for the last twelve years. For me, it is important to think twice before altering nature - Arati Baruah".

References

Hydro Power, "energypedia".

Search "United Nations Sustainable Water and Energy Solutions Network."

https://www.ozy.com/"230000-died-in-a-dam-collapse-that-china-kept-secret-for-years/91699"

Chapter 16

In the United States, in the last century, meandering rivers were straightened out; that is not the

River Engineering

case now. Meandering is accepted both as scientifically and environmentally correct. These concepts brought a new outlook on engineering the rivers.

When a river goes through slopes it has speed and it can take more or less straight path. However, it can go through twists and turns for a lot of different reasons. Straitening, channeling or altering can disrupts many such benefits. Meandering rivers, characterized by their winding, sinuous paths, offer a range of ecological, geological, and societal benefits. The slow flow and connectivity of meandering rivers allow for the sediments to collect at certain sides, it helps movement of aquatic species. Meandering rivers create a variety of habitats, including pools, riffles, and backwaters, which support diverse ecosystems. These habitats can provide homes and breeding grounds for numerous species of fish, birds, and other wildlife.

Meanders act as natural flood control mechanisms. The natural meandering pattern of rivers helps dissipate the energy of floodwaters. This reduces the risk of catastrophic flooding downstream by slowing down and spreading out the flow during heavy rain events or snowmelt. Meanders also allow water to infiltrate the ground. This process helps recharge groundwater supplies, which can be crucial for maintaining water availability in regions that rely on aquifers.

Meandering rivers transport sediments and nutrients downstream, replenishing soils and promoting healthy riparian ecosystems which in turn help sustain deltas and wetlands, which are important for various ecological functions. The slow and winding nature of meandering rivers can help reduce the erosion of riverbanks and adjacent lands. The vegetation along meanders also plays a role in stabilizing banks and preventing erosion.

Meandering rivers can act as natural filters, removing pollutants and excess nutrients from the water as it flows through various habitats. This helps improve water quality downstream. Meandering rivers can help buffer the effects of climate change by providing resilience against extreme weather events such as floods and droughts. They also contribute to carbon storage in riparian vegetation and sediments. The new mindset is to think twice before altering nature.

Reference

McCully, Patrick, "Silenced Rivers, the Ecology and Politics of Large Dams", Zed Books

Search for The US Army Corps of Engineers, Search for successful big projects.

Next Page, Meandering Rivers

Courtesy: US National Park Service. The significance of this is – now we think twice before engineering a river. The salmon looks for certain places to lay eggs, beavers know where to build their dams.

A meandering river

Chapter 17

It can be hard, or even impossible, to take everything into account when trying to solve climate change issues. There is simply a lot to think about, and it is all connected. Oceans are a big part of the world's assets, and their health is a complex subject. Rivers, a source of freshwater, take minerals and salts down to the ocean—we have to take healthy and unhealthy erosion into account. The water cycle, evaporation, clouds,

A Sustainable Earth
and rain are a natural recycling effort. Beyond water, we have to think of plants. Plants bring other nutrients, potassium, calcium, and minerals from the Earth to human beings and other animals. Then, there is weather —scientists can model some of nature's acts but can only simulate others, like predicting storms. Tornadoes and cyclones sometimes form too quickly. These are multivariable problems (for example, pressure, temperature, water content), and all the variables' rates of change are also of concern, making mathematical modeling much harder. Even all this is only the beginning of what the problem of climate change brings to the table.

Climate change brings all disciplines to action, including sciences like physics, chemistry, geology, civil engineering, and botany. Engineering disciplines need to restructure, too, to combine environmental variables. Just like COVID-19, climate change is a wake-up call for humanity. It transcends geological borders, and its geopolitical nature makes it challenging to solve—but not impossible. A clear understanding and good education only can lead to a flourishing, sustainable Earth.

Because these challenges are interdisciplinary, open minds from every world citizen are required. No matter who you are, you can play a part. You do not have to be a scientist but a science-oriented person with a deep respect for Mother Earth. Doctors can stay away from prescribing tons of "magical pills" and let people understand their body better! Artists can do wonderful illustrations of how pollution happens; marketers are already on it by saying that they are organic and environmentally friendly—let's hope they stay honest. Indigenous people show a big example of preserving our Earth! They were very good to earth, neither mining everything nor engineering the rivers wrong way. We need to learn from them!

As I have repeatedly said, climate change knows no borders. We have already seen how changes in weather patterns, such as extreme storms, droughts, or heat waves, impact both neighboring regions and distant areas through interconnected ecosystems and atmospheric circulation. Volcanoes do the same. Without lush forests, the Earth cannot clean up pollution well enough—nature's recycling process is breaking down. It is as simple as that. If this continues to happen, we will have no choice but to settle for nature's fury! Different countries have different priorities, interests, and levels of development, and, combined with short-term economic considerations, these do not foster progress globally. Climate conferences by the United Nations are merely awareness and education. Even though everybody's skin is in the game, countries are still more worried about security and money than they are about moral obligations and environmental justice.

How the next fifty years will play out depends on having young, educated, solid leaders worldwide. Even simple things like planting community gardens, supporting companies that prioritize environmentally friendly practices and products, and developing strategies will help a lot. We can conserve energy and water, reduce waste, and use eco-friendly products and packaging. We can work on cleaner energy.

Chapter 18

No matter what, large climate changes are coming —indeed, they are

How to be Prepared

alreay here. So, how can we prepare ourselves? The first step is awareness of your particular situation, and education of the situation worldwide.

Look around the natural surroundings where you live. What kind of topology does the land you are living in have? Is it highland or lowland? Could it endure twenty-four hours of incessant rain? If it is a lowland, it can have flash floods. If it is a highland, you can have erosion because the ground is soaked. Similar things can happen if you are near the bank of a small creek.

If you live by the ocean, look for coral health in any nearby coral reef. Good coral health is a good sign for us! Coral reefs help break up storms and are a sign of healthy ocean life. How much do you know about your coastal lands? Think about the areas in the Louisiana coast, where people are already displaced. In lowlands around Florida, water is leaking on the roads. Are you buying property there? If so, do you have a plan for when this gets worse? If not, could something similar happen to you?

Do you live on barrier islands? They break up the storms, just like coral reefs. Keep the barrier islands healthy!

We all live downstream of one or even several rivers. Keep good track of what's happening upstream of all nearby rivers by getting involved in volunteering activities of city and state parks. We need rivers to be healthy and natural. Remember, a healthy river floods, but we want it to happen within some limits if we can. Leave enough land near the rivers as a cushion!

No matter who you are or where you live, you must work on developing a tremendous sense of being linked to nature.

Keep a good updated on glacier melting all over the world. It is a benchmark of our planet's health.

Be wary of animal populations, and do not participate in the consumption of animals that are overfished or rare. In 2021 and 2022, king crab fishing had a devastating effect—billions of king crab vanished in the Bering Sea of Alaska. The last two Eastern Bering Sea trawl surveys (in 2021 and 2022) indicated a continuing decline in Alaska red king crabs, with female levels falling so low they had to close the fishery. Similarly, Maine lobster fishermen are struggling with declining lobster populations and consequent industry challenges.

Stay tuned for all kinds of issues that are going to cause chain reactions in the community—education is paramount to ensure you are not participating in harmful cycles.

Annual mean temperature over northern Canada increased by roughly three times the global mean warming rate. Note that the global average of temperature rise is 2° degree cCelsius. The rate is at least three times higher near the poles than at the equator, that's why ice caps and glaciers are already starting to melt.

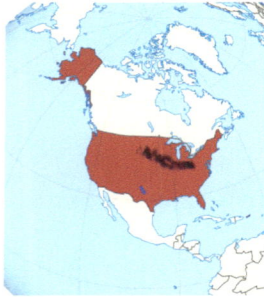

American side of the globe

Do a thought experiment. Imagine the Himalayan mountain range showed on the Eurasian side of the globe (Chapter on Jet Streams) on top of the Great Lakes in the map of the USA. Remember, it is a hypothetical scenario, impossible to be built by humans. Try to think, will the climate change drastically? This example is selected because, without knowing it, humans sometimes alter natural topography. When the damages are realized, it is too late. Also, different countries do different things —some are gentle on Nature, some are not. Engineers can get crazy with heavy equipment and build roads up in the mountain peaks where they should not be built because the soil could be erosion-prone, making mudslides!

Eurasian side of the globe.

Yes, the climate will change by replacing the lakes with a lofty, long mountain range, but there will be other consequences. Probably, the Arctic blast will be gone or diminished. No more cold air from the North Pole or Canada to make winter unbearable with blizzards and heavy snow. It will be blocked by "the fake Himalayas of the US." Chicago will no longer be a windy city. When the polar jet stream meanders southward across the United States, the cold polar air can push as far south as Texas and the Gulf Coast. Cold Arctic air can spill southward to mid-latitudes when the polar jet stream develops a wavier or meandering pattern. This phenomenon is commonly known as Artic Blast. Arctic blasts, also known as Arctic air outbreaks or cold fronts, are weather phenomena that bring freezing and cold air from the

Arctic region southward into mid-latitude areas, including North America. A rapid temperature drop characterizes these events and often brings strong winds and sometimes snow or freezing precipitation.

The Himalayan Wall mountain range is way taller than the Great Wall of China and impossible to be built by humans. The Great Wall of China is 0.9 miles at the highest spot (on mountain Huanglouwa, 80 miles NW of Beijing). Note that the High Himalayas range is five miles high! Since the high and long "Himalayas" will trap moist air, there will be plenty of rain near the "Himalayas," but there will be a rain shadow behind. So, north of these "Himalayas" will be barren soon. The consequences of such an action would depend on the time of year, the specific meteorological conditions, and the magnitude of the Arctic blast.

Here is a list of what the weather might look like in the US Midwest point by point.

The most immediate effect would likely be an increase in temperatures. Arctic blasts bring frigid air masses, so temperatures would likely be milder without one.

Arctic blasts often bring snow and ice to the Midwest. Without the explosion, there would be less snowfall and ice accumulation. Less snowfall could impact winter sports and snow-related industries.

Arctic blasts can lead to stormy weather with strong winds and heavy precipitation. Without them, the Midwest might experience more stable and calmer weather patterns.

Altering the weather patterns in one region can have ripple effects on climate and weather patterns in adjacent areas. It might lead to more extreme weather events in other parts of the continent.

The US Midwest is a central agricultural region. Changes in weather patterns could have significant implications for crops, affecting planting and harvesting schedules as well as crop yields. Farmers may have to cultivate a whole different types of crops.

Changes in temperature and weather patterns could also impact local ecosystems and wildlife, potentially disrupting migration patterns and food availability.

With milder temperatures there might be reduced demand for heating during the winter, impacting energy consumption and costs.

We have seen that tampering with natural weather patterns can have unintended consequences and potentially disrupt the delicate balance of the Earth's climate system. Weather systems are interconnected; altering one part can lead to unforeseen impacts elsewhere. Additionally, the technology to control or prevent weather events on such a large scale does not currently exist, and any attempt to do so would have profound ethical, environmental, and scientific implications.

As we have learned in the chapter "Jet Streams," arctic blasts are polar jets originating in the Arctic region, encompassing the North Pole and the surrounding areas. During the winter months, the Arctic experiences continuous darkness and extreme cold. High-pressure systems can develop over this region, leading to the accumulation of icy air.

In the USA, meteorologists closely monitor these events, and advance warning is often provided to help people prepare for the extreme cold and associated weather conditions.

But remember, these are examples you write with a caveat. Besides, one can't predict everything; there could be more unintended consequences. But please agree that mountains as high as the Himalayas will change climates drastically. It is the same way with oceans. If climate change continues too long, we will have drastic environmental changes. Some places will become deserts! We have not studied the effect of the Himalayas on global weather. We eventually need to do this. We will retouch this example in the Chapter "Nature is a Slow Large-Scale Builder."

This imaginary exercise would help to realize how the Himalayas control climate worldwide. The Amazon forests and the Himalayas are critical to climate study—they are even more important than you realize. Keep thinking about what mountains do versus plain lands.

The Chinese balloon that trespassed the US in February 2023 was moved by the jet stream, at least in its final phase, from Montana to North Carolina. This fact should make the subtropical jet stream a reality in your mind and easier to understand. We do not see the jet streams, but we can see its action and how it pushed the balloon around a specific path. Meteorologists and scientists used computer models incorporating data on wind patterns, weather conditions, and the balloon's characteristics to predict its trajectory. These models provide forecasts of where the balloon will travel over time. The US was correct in predicting where it would leave the land area and blew it away precisely as soon as it got over the ocean.

Let us take another journey in this thought path. Will the Great Salt Lake of Utah become like Owen Lake of California? Because of the average temperature rise and draught consequences, it could happen. If you follow this development, you will be preparing yourself for a climate crisis. Here is what happened to Owens Lake. Owens Lake is a primarily dried-up lake in the valley of the eastern side of the Sierra Nevada in California. Little water remains. Historically, the Owens River used to flow into Owens Lake, providing a water source for the lake. However, in the early 20th century, Los Angeles implemented an extensive water diversion project that redirected water from the Owens River and other nearby sources to supply the growing city. This diversion severely reduced water flow into Owens Lake, leading to a significant drop in lake levels. The shrinking water levels in Owens Lake exposed vast expanses of lakebeds that were rich in fine dusty sediments. The dry lakebed became a significant source of airborne dust, especially during windy conditions. This dust pollution had profound air quality implications for the region. As a result of lawsuits and legal actions by environmental groups, the city of Los Angeles was forced to address the dust pollution problem and comply with air quality standards. It led to a series of actions to control dust emissions, including flooding certain lakebed areas to create shallow, saline ponds and implementing dust control measures.

Think—is your local lake on the same path? Let's take Utah's Great Salt Lake, for example. Owens and Great Salt Lake are terminal (or "endorheic") lakes, meaning no rivers come from them. Rivers have this dynamic mechanism of taking minerals away down to the ocean. Terminal lakes collect minerals, sometimes heavy metals, and other substances without an outlet.

The truth is that the Great Salt Lake is drying up; if we do not act immediately, it will be a dust bed. Being endorheic for billions of years, it has selenium, mercury, arsenic, and other human-friendly and unfriendly materials. If it is dried, dust storms will carry these materials into the air, killing nearby residents and polluting the air for an extensive area.

What can be done? The answer is do not let these terminal lakes dry up or find alternatives to hide arsenic! Again, do not change Nature unless you are convinced there will be no dire consequences.

Chapter 19

Temperature of our palnet is rising everywhere. The Mediterranean Sea is showing an estimated warming of about one degree Celsius over the last three decades (according to data collection by Copernicus). In the summer of 2023, in Southern Europe it felt as if North Africa had moved to the Mediterranean. Portugal and Spain were as hot as Arizona (over 100°F for over a month). The Gulf

Temperature is Rising Everywhere

of Mexico is also warming with an alarming rate per decade—warming is occurring at all depths. In Florida, Manatee Bay surface water is heating to a record 100°F. These were in the news lately. These are not just statistics; they are reality. We all need to cut our carbon footprints by taking public transportation when we can and encourage corporations to take up clean energy, to mention a couple.

Know the native plants of your forests. Do not import many foreign plants to your native forest without considering or knowing new species' adaptation to the climate. Importing Eucalyptus to Portugal and replacing the native forests with this Eucalyptus recently caused enormous wildfires. Consider planting local plants in your yard instead of foreign plants or grass. They will do better in your climate and help support local wildlife.

If we do not have food on our table, we cannot think of saving the planet. Everybody in the world is responsible for the climate change but we cannot just do finger pointing about who is the It is a hard realization we do not control or affect only our geographical part of the atmosphere.

This is not an exhaustive discussion but an attempt to show things that you can explore yourself to gauge climate change and find the best way you can help. As you learn, make your list. And remember, climate change knows no borders. To be a world citizen is hard. To be aware of international issues, we need education. This may sound repetitive, but this is the only way to get this in our head. "Save the planet" is not only a slogan— it must become our way of life!

2023 September was the hottest one ever and 2023 is firmly set to be the warmest year on record, the World Meteorological Organization (WMO) said, citing data from the

European Union's Copernicus Climate Change Service (C3S).1

Reference

Mediterranean Temperature Reference: **Europe's** Copernicus Data Space Ecosystem

Chapter 20

Current climate change, an impending global crisis, is not an adversary one can escape. The notion of ignoring its effects is a futile undertaking. To confront this threat, we must gather the collective will to address the root causes and take decisive action to cleanse our planet's atmosphere. It is like the statement, "You can run away, but there is no place to hide."

Can You Run Away from Climate Change? - A Comprehensive Summary

Two undeniable facts highlight the urgency of the climate change problem. First, there is a continuous surge in carbon dioxide (CO_2) levels in our atmosphere. Though CO_2 constitutes a mere 0.04 percent of our atmosphere today, the startling reality is that Earth's atmospheric CO_2 has increased by 50 percent since the onset of the Industrial Revolution. This surge has pushed CO_2 levels to unprecedented heights in millions of years.

However, it's essential to recognize that the problem extends beyond CO_2 alone. It encompasses a broader increase in greenhouse gases, which includes not just CO_2 but also nitrous oxide (NO), methane (CH_4), and ozone (O_3). These greenhouse gases collectively contribute to the rise in global temperatures.

The delicate balance of Earth's ecosystems plays a pivotal role in mitigating the impact of greenhouse gases. Humans, for instance, exhale carbon dioxide, while plants absorb this CO_2 and reciprocate by releasing oxygen. Animals of all kinds, water, the sun's energy – or just Nature - get into this ecosystem equation. Maintaining a healthy ecosystem is crucial for regulating and refreshing carbon dioxide levels, emphasizing our interdependence with the natural world.

Some skeptics argue that we have been warned about impending ice ages, suggesting that climate change may be just another phase in a natural cycle. However, climate change, as we currently experience it, is an unprecedented challenge. It represents an uncharted territory for humanity, with potentially unforeseen consequences. We cannot rely on past patterns to predict the future accurately. The Earth is going through a giant new experiment.

The scientific consensus tells us that the focus should now be on restraining the rise in global temperatures to a target of 1.5 degrees Celsius above pre-industrial levels. As elaborated throughout this book, achieving this goal necessitates profoundly modifying our energy systems, consumption patterns, and policies.

The climate crisis is a touching reminder that escaping the grips of climate change is not an option. Instead, we must confront this global challenge head-on, taking unwavering steps to reduce greenhouse gas emissions, protect our ecosystems, and strive for a sustainable future. Only by facing the issue with solid determination can we hope to mitigate the devastating effects of climate change and secure a habitable planet for future generations.

Carbon dioxide (CO_2) and pollution are environmental issues that should be significant ecological concerns. However, it's essential to understand their specific implications and distinctions; they have different impacts and implications. Carbon dioxide is a crucial driver of climate change, which has far-reaching consequences for the planet's climate system. Pollution, on the other hand, encompasses a wide range of harmful substances that can directly harm human health and the environment. Both issues require attention and concerted efforts to mitigate their adverse effects and work toward a more sustainable and healthier planet. The ranking of worst polluters can change over time depending on the specific metric used, carbon dioxide and/or methane, the time frame, and per capita emissions. Cities in countries with less stringent environmental regulations may have inferior air quality. Plastic pollution is a global concern, and so is deforestation.

Some look for other celestial bodies for extra resources. There are plans and ambitions to send astronauts to the Moon for long-duration missions, including establishing lunar bases or habitats. NASA's long-term goal is to establish a sustainable presence on the Moon by early 2030s. NASA is working with international partners, including the European Space Agency (ESA), the Canadian Space Agency (CSA), and others, to achieve its lunar goals. Russia's Roscosmos, China's CNSA, and India's ISRO have also expressed interest in lunar exploration and habitation. USA, Russia, China, and India have already landed spacecraft on the Moon's surface.

There are many technical, logistical, and financial challenges to overcome before humans can establish a sustained presence on the Moon; one is extreme temperature variation within a lunar day. Lunar surface temperatures range from hot (127 degrees Celsius or 260 degrees Fahrenheit) during lunar day to cold (-173 degrees Celsius or -280 degrees Fahrenheit) during lunar night.

So, the moral is to reduce your carbon footprint.

References
Educators 4SC
https://educators4sc.org/teaching-about-affordable-and-clean-energy/

> **A carbon footprint is the total amount of greenhouse gases (carbon dioxide and methane) generated by our actions.**

Chapter 21

A profound assertion is that Nature acts as an extensive constructor, with its building endeavors intricately connected to the fundamental processes and principles of physics. We need to realize this before we alter Nature. Mountains rise, and continents shift due to the slow movement of tec-

Nature is a Slow Large Scale Builder

tonic plates over millions of years. Erosion carves out landscapes, and rivers create intricate networks, all through gradual, persistent actions. Nature is a grand-scale builder, engineer, physicist and maintainer. The statement reflects the remarkable ability of natural processes and systems to create, shape, and sustain the world around us. Over history, we learned that new diseases happened when people dramatically changed their lifestyles. We are still inviting new epidemics. Man and microbes have gone through mutual adaptation.

Animals played their role, too. Understanding the slowness of natural processes helps us appreciate the significance of conservation efforts, as the damage caused by human activities often outpaces the ability of nature to rebuild and restore itself. Additionally, it highlights the need for long-term thinking and sustainable practices to protect the environment and its intricate systems.

We can dive deeper into this idea to explore how Nature functions as an architect and builder on a grand scale. The following list of natural processes is based on shared knowledge and a general understanding of how Nature shapes the environment.

Geological processes are the most prominent example of Nature's building prowess. Over millions of years, natural forces like tectonic plate movements, erosion, and volcanic activity have constructed vast mountain ranges, deep ocean trenches, and extensive plains, plateaus, and valleys. Rift valleys are still popping up throughout the world. The Himalayas are home to diverse flora and fauna, including the endangered snow leopard and the rare blue poppy. The Mariana Trench, located in the western Pacific Ocean, is the deepest point on Earth, where extreme pressure and darkness create unique habitats for creatures such as the giant tube worm and the anglerfish. The Serengeti Plain is one of the world's most extensive and productive grasslands, where millions of wildebeest, zebra, and antelope migrate annually for food and water. Geological processes shape the Earth and influence the diversity and distribution of life. Geological time scales demonstrate the slowness of natural processes.

Next Page:

A bird's-eye view of a gorge in the East African Rift at Engaruka, Tanzania. (Image credit: Ulrich Doering/Alamy)

A piece of East Africa may break off the main continent in tens of millions of years. East Africa's Rift Valley

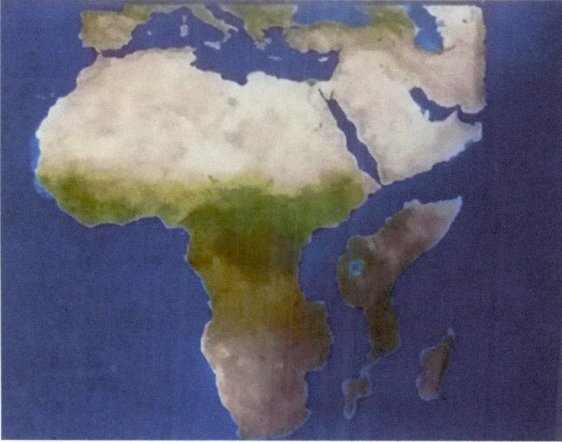

In distant geological time East Africa
may split like this!

Nature is a master at creating diverse eco-systems. From lush rainforests teeming with bio-diversity to arid deserts that support unique life forms, ecosystems are intricate designs that result from the interplay of climate, geology, and biol-ogy. Each ecosystem has specialized builders, such as beavers constructing dams or coral reefs grow-ing over centuries, shaping their surroundings.

Nature's building ability is perhaps most evi-dent in evolution. Through natural selection, organisms have evolved over billions of years, adapting to their environments and coexisting with other species. The change process, which has given rise to the incredible diversity of life on Earth, is slow and incremental. It takes countless generations for species to adapt to their environ-ments, leading to development of new traits and species over vast periods.

Climate systems shape entire regions, driven by the Earth's position and rotation. Natural weather patterns, such as the water cycle, produce rainfall, nourishing landscapes, forming rivers, and even carving out breathtaking canyons over time. Bio-logical climate change processes, such as ice ages and interglacial periods, operate on timescales of tens of thousands to millions of years. Earlier in the book, we have gone through details of air movement, including jet systems. The weathering and erosion of rocks and landscapes by wind, water, and ice occur slowly but continuously. It can take millions of years for significant changes in landforms to become apparent.

The world's oceans are colossal builders in their own right. They regulate Earth's temperature, store massive amounts of carbon, and provide a habitat for countless marine species. Coral reefs, in particular, are incredible structures built by tiny coral polyps over millennia. These reefs provide habitat for numerous aquatic species.

Nature creates valuable minerals and resources. Mountains and volcanic activity are instrumental in forming minerals, while fossilization processes have preserved the history of life in the form of fossils. Creating fertile soil through the breakdown of rocks, the accumulation of organic matter, and the action of microorganisms is a slow process that can take centuries to millennia.

Fossil Fuel Formation: Fossil fuels like coal, oil, and natural gas, which power much of the world, are the remnants of ancient plants and organisms that slowly decomposed and transformed over millions of years under pressure and heat

Making of Trees Jungles and Forests: Their growth can span decades to centuries, from a tiny seed to a towering tree. They play a critical role in carbon sequestration and ecosystem stability. Nature plays a vital role in regulating the composition of our atmosphere. Plants, through photosynthesis, produce oxygen and absorb carbon dioxide, helping to maintain the delicate balance necessary for supporting life on Earth.

Even on a cosmic scale, Nature has shaped our planet. The formation of Earth itself, its position in the solar system, and the influence of celestial bodies like the Moon have all contributed to the unique conditions that make life possible here.

Nature's processes encapsulate the idea that natural processes and systems have shaped our planet, its landscapes, ecosystems, and life forms on an immense scale. From geological formations to the intricate web of life, the Earth is a testament to the extraordinary building capabilities of Nature, which continues to shape and evolve our world to this day. Recognizing and respecting this builder's role can inspire greater appreciation and conservation efforts to safeguard our planet and its natural wonders. Nature humbles our engineering endeavors and provides a necessary perspective, and only understanding Nature will make humans survive in this critical moment. It's important to note that tampering with natural patterns can have unintended consequences and potentially disrupt the delicate balance of the Earth's integrated system. All systems are interconnected; altering one part can lead to unforeseen impacts elsewhere. The technology to control or prevent floods and other weather events on such a large scale does not currently exist, and any attempt to do so would have profound ethical, environmental, and scientific implications.

We need to realize this while doing Mega or

Giga-dams—Giga dams harm by altering, actually drowning, a vast extent of the area. The Himalayas are the world's youngest mountain and are geologically active. The tectonic plates' movement is not as dramatic as in the case of East Africa's Rift Valley or when the Himalayas were formed forty million years ago. But Mount Everest is still rising by half of an inch every year. The ultimate consequence of Africa's rift valley is the creation of a new ocean in the distant future. This rift area is associated with volcanic activity; a famous example is Mount Kilimanjaro. The positive effect now is it is rich in geothermal energy. It is also an earthquake-prone area. However, the local people must adapt to changing landscapes, resources, and potential hazards. This example is more visual and helps us think of Nature's building process, whether it is less apparent or more intuitive.

References

Search for "Koppen-geiger Climate Classifications"

Chapter 22

Fusion, the process by which the Sun generates energy, is now possible in the laboratory. It takes time to engineer it into a real working process, but once we do, we will be able to create energy with much less waste, much less use of fossil fuels, and much less pollution. It is truly a ray of

A Ray of Hope

hope. Nuclear fusion is the opposite of nuclear fission, and with its advent, the world may be able to get rid of potentially destructive nuclear power! We look forward to the process of nuclear fusion, it is likely to happen very soon. Fusion remains a promising clean and virtually limitless energy source, and ongoing research and development efforts continue to move us closer to achieving this goal. It is a challenging task, new insights into plasma physics, materials science, and other related fields can lead to more efficient fusion reactor designs and operational techniques. There is hope. A pollution-free world take a team effort, and sometimes such a budget is not a priority. We have to make it a priority. The future is not bleak, with proper mindset clean energy will be possible.

Index

Dr. Arati Bora Baruah, a retired Senior Specialist Engineer with a remarkable 35-year tenure at Boeing, spent the last decade of her career as a flight test engineer. Hailing from Guwahati, India, she received her education from local institutions such as Cotton College and Guwahati University before pursuing further studies in the USA at Indiana University, Bloomington, and later at the University of Washington, Seattle, where she earned her Ph.D. in Electrical Engineering.

As a "loaned executive," Boeing entrusted her to serve as a professor at a local engineering college for two years, and she continued as an adjunct professor for an additional decade. The majority of her professional journey unfolded at Boeing.

In the past decade, Dr. Baruah has dedicated herself to addressing water issues in India and combating global warming through extensive research and the application of her scientific expertise. Following her retirement from

Boeing, her notable achievements include studying the circular nature of the Brahmaputra River using models, substantiating reasons against linking the Teesta, Santosh, and Manas rivers, investigating manmade floods in Guwahati, and contributing articles to Amar Asom on subjects like the Subansiri Dam and the potential hazards of constructing mega dams for hydroelectricity in the Eastern Himalayas, particularly due to the soft-soil nature of the region. Additionally, she has explained flooding dynamics in terms of rivers accumulating silt and sedimentation.

In the realm of communications technology, Dr. Baruah made a significant impact by being an early and vocal advocate for the Assamese Unicode standard. She has authored books in English and also in her native language of Assam.

www.ingramcontent.com/pod-product-compliance
Lightning Source LLC
Chambersburg PA
CBHW041917260326
41914CB00013B/1478